# Contents

D1739392

I trust that this illustrated guide facilitates identification, use and care of foliage and will encourage you to be more adventurous in the use of design and concept.

Foliage is not just "Greens"! Although that may have been the belief years ago, this concept seems to persist with some florists today, as well as with the customers. If customers think that foliage grows for free in the hedgerows, they should be informed otherwise. Hedgerows are anyway rare enough these days.

Foliage is commercially grown all over the world and should be treated in the same way as flowers. It is grown and harvested the same as flowers and should therefore be charged for as with flowers. Africa, Australia, India, Sri Lanka, North, South and Central America as well as Europe are main growing areas and many a family's income depends on it.

It is obviously impractical to give foliage away when it has to be purchased and why leave your valuable foliage in a bucket in the corner and wait until a customer asks for some. Clever use of foliage will not only increase florist's profitability in itself but make flower arrangements, handtieds and most floristry work much more interesting, provide more texture and give the impression of space. Use it as a value added item to boost your sales and be different from the competition!

Please note that not all the foliages listed in this book are true foliages. Whilst the list of foliages is intended to be the main commercial foliages, there may be a small number ommited that will be added to reprints as they become available. Sizes of bunches and length vary from supplier to supplier, measurements given are only an indication.

Please also note that it is unrealistic to expect foliages which are grown in the wild such as Arbutus, Bay, Salal and others to be completely perfect, nature is always a compromise. Any irregularities and variations are in no way to be considered as defective, what should be looked for is the overall impact.

I would like to express my gratitude to Dudley Button who has succeeded in capturing the main features of the foliages on photograph and has been a great help and encouragement to produce this book. Thanks are also due to Kevin Davies for his untiring work in achieving the agreed layout in spite of endless revisions.

*Veronika Strong.*
*Evesham. September 1996*

Veronika Strong  Foliage for Florists
Published by Strong's Greenery © 1996

**STEPPING STONES**
INTO THE UNKNOWN LTD
P.O. BOX 108
EVESHAM
WR11 5ZL

| | |
|---|---|
| **BOTANICAL NAME** | *Abelia* |
| **FAMILY NAME** | *Caprifoliaceae* |
| **COMMON NAME** | *Abelia* |

**AVAILABILITY** ● September - July

**DESCRIPTION** ● Shiny, dark purple-to-green, small ovate leaves on slender woody stem.

**USES** ● Handtieds, pedestals, line emphasis.

**CARE POINTS** ● Re-cut & put into clean water, no additives. Put in a cool ventilated but not drafty place.

# *Abies grandis*

| | |
|---|---|
| **BOTANICAL NAME** | *Abies grandis* |
| **FAMILY NAME** | *Pinaceae* |
| **COMMON NAME** | *Grand fir* |

---

| | | |
|---|---|---|
| **AVAILABILITY** | ● | Winter months. |
| **DESCRIPTION** | ● | Green, more open needles on flat branch |
| **USES** | ● | Christmas and funeral work. |
| **CARE POINTS** | ● | Keep cool for prompt use - if to be kept longer recut and put into clean water. |

**Abies nobilis**

| | |
|---|---|
| BOTANICAL NAME | *Abies nobilis* |
| FAMILY NAME | *Pinaceae* |
| COMMON NAME | *Blue pine, silver fir* |

| | | |
|---|---|---|
| AVAILABILITY | ● | November - December |
| DESCRIPTION | ● | Blue-ish thick needles on stem. |
| USES | ● | Arrangements, baskets, funerals, Christmas decorations. |
| CARE POINTS | ● | Keep cool. |

# Acacia

| | |
|---|---|
| **BOTANICAL NAME** | *Acacia* |
| **FAMILY NAME** | *Leguminoseae* |
| **COMMON NAME** | *Mimosa* |

| | | |
|---|---|---|
| **AVAILABILITY** | ● | January - March |
| **DESCRIPTION** | ● | Feathery, sensitive leaves much branched on woody stem. |
| **USES** | ● | Arrangements, handtieds & designer work. |
| **CARE POINTS** | ● | Re-cut stems & put into clean water, no additives.  Put in a cool ventilated but not drafty place. |

| | |
|---|---|
| **BOTANICAL NAME** | *Acacia pravisima* |
| **FAMILY NAME** | *Leguminoseae* |
| **COMMON NAME** | *Knife edge acacia, Saw tooth acacia* |

| | | |
|---|---|---|
| **AVAILABILITY** | ● | All year |
| **DESCRIPTION** | ● | Distinctive triangular leaves closely on stem. |
| **USES** | ● | Trailing & designer work, line emphasis. |
| **CARE POINTS** | ● | Cut off 2 inches & put into clean water. Use promptly. Do not store for any length of time. |

# *Aglaonema silver*

| | |
|---|---|
| **BOTANICAL NAME** | *Aglaonema silver* |
| **FAMILY NAME** | *Araceae* |
| **COMMON NAME** | *Aglaonema* |

| | | |
|---|---|---|
| **AVAILABILITY** | ● | All year |
| **DESCRIPTION** | ● | Medium variegated ovate shaped leaves with green edges. |
| **USES** | ● | Arrangements, baskets, handtieds, line emphasis. |
| **CARE POINTS** | ● | Wrap in plastic & put in a cool place. |

**_Alchemilla mollis_**

| | |
|---|---|
| BOTANICAL NAME | *Alchemilla mollis* |
| FAMILY NAME | *Rosaceae* |
| COMMON NAME | *Ladies mantle* |

| | | |
|---|---|---|
| AVAILABILITY | ● | May - June |
| DESCRIPTION | ● | Lime green dainty tufts of florets on green stem, encircled by serated green leaves. |
| USES | ● | Arrangements, baskets, handtieds, pedestals, funeral work.  Filler & colour emphasis. |
| CARE POINTS | ● | Re-cut & put into clean water with flower food. |

## Alpinia zerumbei 'variegata'

| | |
|---|---|
| **BOTANICAL NAME** | *Alpinia zerumbei 'variegata'* |
| **FAMILY NAME** | *Ziugiberaceae* |
| **COMMON NAME** | *Variegated ginger* |

| | | |
|---|---|---|
| **AVAILABILITY** | ● | All year |
| **DESCRIPTION** | ● | Medium sized, oval single leaves heavily variegated in yellow & green. |
| **USES** | ● | Arrangements, baskets, designer work, underlining design. |
| **CARE POINTS** | ● | Keep misted, wrapped loosely in plastic. Upside down. Keep in a cool place (5°C). Use promptly. |

| BOTANICAL NAME | *Amaranthus* |
|---|---|
| FAMILY NAME | *Amaranthaceae* |
| COMMON NAME | *Love-lies bleeding* |

| | | |
|---|---|---|
| AVAILABILITY | ● | May - September |
| DESCRIPTION | ● | Erect or droopy thick flower clusters on soft stem. Available in lime green or dark red. |
| USES | ● | Designer work, handties, pedestals, arrangements, line & colour emphasis. |
| CARE POINTS | ● | Strip off bigger leaves & re-cut into fresh water, add flower food. Use promptly. Dries well. |

| | |
|---|---|
| **BOTANICAL NAME** | *Ananus stirus* |
| **FAMILY NAME** | *Bromelidaceae* |
| **COMMON NAME** | *Love pines / love cones* |

**AVAILABILITY** ● All year.

**DESCRIPTION** ● Baby pineapple on erect stem.

**USES** ● Novelty and focal point.

**CARE POINTS** ● Keep dry and cool.

*Anethum graveolens*

| | |
|---|---|
| **BOTANICAL NAME** | *Anethum graveolens* |
| **FAMILY NAME** | *Umbelliferae* |
| **COMMON NAME** | *Dill* |

**AVAILABILITY** ● All year

**DESCRIPTION** ● A light green feathery & aromatic foliage with distinct seed head. (Used as a herb).

**USES** ● Handtieds, arrangements.

**CARE POINTS** ● Re-cut & put into clean water.

| BOTANICAL NAME | *Anthurium leaves* |
|---|---|
| FAMILY NAME | *Araceae* |
| COMMON NAME | *Leaves of flamingo flower* |

| | | |
|---|---|---|
| AVAILABILITY | ● | All year |
| DESCRIPTION | ● | Medium to large heart shaped green leaves with stem at angle. 20-30cm long. |
| USES | ● | Arrangements, pedestals & designer work. |
| CARE POINTS | ● | Keep misted, wrapped loosely in plastic. Keep in a cool place (5°C). Use promptly.  Avoid rough handling. |

## Arachniodes adiantiformis

| | |
|---|---|
| **BOTANICAL NAME** | *Arachniodes adiantiformis* (Central America)<br>*Rumohra adiantiformis* (African) |
| **FAMILY NAME** | *Aspidaceae* |
| **COMMON NAME** | *Leather leaf* |

**AVAILABILITY** ● All year

**DESCRIPTION** ● Large triangular fern on main stem.

**USES** ● All floristry work.

**CARE POINTS** ● Keep misted, wrapped loosely in plastic.
Keep in a cool place (5°C).
Use promptly. Do not unwrap & put into water.

# Aralia

| BOTANICAL NAME | *Aralia* |
|---|---|
| FAMILY NAME | *Araliaceae* |
| COMMON NAME | *Castor oil plant, Angelica tree* |

**AVAILABILITY** ● All year

**DESCRIPTION** ● Green & variegated, hand-shaped leaves, 15cm - 30cm across.

**USES** ● Arrangements, handtieds & underlining design.

**CARE POINTS** ● Keep misted in plastic in a cool place (5°C). Day before use re-cut & put into clean water, no additives. If limp submerge into water for a few hours.

| | |
|---|---|
| **BOTANICAL NAME** | *Arbutus unedo* |
| **FAMILY NAME** | *Ericaceae* |
| **COMMON NAME** | *Strawberry tree* |

**AVAILABILITY** ● August - November

**DESCRIPTION** ● Woody stem with reddish bark, evergreen glossy foliage, oval & slightly serrated leaves.

**USES** ● Bouquets, handtieds, larger arrangements, pedestals.

**CARE POINTS** ● Re-cut & put into clean water, no additives. Keep in cool place.

## Asparagus meyeri

| | |
|---|---|
| **BOTANICAL NAME** | *Asparagus meyeri* |
| **FAMILY NAME** | *Liliaceae* |
| **COMMON NAME** | *Foxtail* |

**AVAILABILITY** ● All year

**DESCRIPTION** ● Upright stems covered with fur-like foliage, hence the name Foxtail.

**USES** ● Arrangements, baskets, wedding & designer work.

**CARE POINTS** ● Keep misted, wrapped loosely in plastic. Keep in a cool place (5°C). Use promptly.

*Asparagus myriocladus*

| | |
|---|---|
| BOTANICAL NAME | *Asparagus myriocladus* |
| FAMILY NAME | *Liliaceae* |
| COMMON NAME | *Ming fern* |

| | | |
|---|---|---|
| AVAILABILITY | ● | All year |
| DESCRIPTION | ● | Tiny tufts of fur on a slender stem with many branches. |
| USES | ● | All floristry work, focal, underlining & filler. |
| CARE POINTS | ● | Keep misted, wrapped loosely in plastic. Keep in a cool place (5°C).  Use promptly. |

# Asparagus plumosus

| | |
|---|---|
| **BOTANICAL NAME** | *Asparagus plumosus* |
| **FAMILY NAME** | *Liliaceae* |
| **COMMON NAME** | *Wedding fern* |

| | | |
|---|---|---|
| **AVAILABILITY** | ● | All year |
| **DESCRIPTION** | ● | Delicate fern in triangle shape on wiry stem. Different length i.e. buttonhole, medium & trailing - up to 1m length. |
| **USES** | ● | Handtieds, pedestals, wedding & designer work, waterfalls, line emphasis. |
| **CARE POINTS** | ● | Keep misted, wrapped loosely in plastic. Keep in a cool place (5°C). Use promptly. |

## Asparagus 'Blue Flame'

| | |
|---|---|
| **BOTANICAL NAME** | *Asparagus pyramidalis 'Blue Flame'* |
| **FAMILY NAME** | *Liliaceae* |
| **COMMON NAME** | *Blue flame* |

| | | |
|---|---|---|
| **AVAILABILITY** | ● | All year |
| **DESCRIPTION** | ● | Long trails with intermittant wild looking tufts of fern on wiry stem. |
| **USES** | ● | All trailing work, handtieds, waterfalls & water scenes. |
| **CARE POINTS** | ● | Keep misted, wrapped loosely in plastic. Put in a cool place (5°C). |

'Blue Flame' is the registered trade mark of some US Ferneries

# *Asparagus smilax*

| | |
|---|---|
| **BOTANICAL NAME** | *Asparagus asparagoides smilax* |
| **FAMILY NAME** | *Liliaceae* |
| **COMMON NAME** | *Smilax* |

**AVAILABILITY** ● May/June - October
(Weather dependant, needs sun)

**DESCRIPTION** ● Slender twiner, hardy. Sold by length,
1 - 3m lengths.

**USES** ● Trailing, wedding work and garlands.

**CARE POINTS** ● Keep misted, wrapped loosely in plastic and
keep in a cool place (5°C).

| BOTANICAL NAME | *Asparagus sprengeri* |
| --- | --- |
| FAMILY NAME | *Liliaceae* |
| COMMON NAME | *Sprengeri* |

AVAILABILITY ● All year

DESCRIPTION ● Wild looking trailing fern, soft needle-like leaves on wiry stem, hidden thorns.

USES ● Designer, wedding & trailing work, pedestals, waterfalls.

CARE POINTS ● Keep misted, wrapped loosley in plastic. Keep in a cool place (5°C). Use promptly.

# *Asparagus virgatus*

| | |
|---|---|
| BOTANICAL NAME | *Asparagus virgatus* |
| FAMILY NAME | *Liliaceae* |
| COMMON NAME | *Treefern* |

| | | |
|---|---|---|
| AVAILABILITY | ● | All year |
| DESCRIPTION | ● | Crown of feathery foliage. On straight stem. |
| USES | ● | Handtieds, posies, wedding work. Foliage to give a 'light' texture and space. |
| CARE POINTS | ● | Keep misted, wrapped loosley in plastic. Keep in a cool place (5°C). Use promptly. |

| | |
|---|---|
| **BOTANICAL NAME** | *Aspidistra* |
| **FAMILY NAME** | *Liliaceae* |
| **COMMON NAME** | *Cast iron plant* |

**AVAILABILITY** ● All year

**DESCRIPTION** ● Green, variegated & Milky Way. Oblong green single leaves or green with cream stripes, 30 -50cm.  Milky way smaller leaves , 10 -15cm, with star-like cream dots.

**USES** ● Arrangements, handtieds, wedding & underlining work.

**CARE POINTS** ● Keep misted, wrapped loosely in plastic.
Keep in a cool place (5°C)

# Aucuba japonica

| | |
|---|---|
| **BOTANICAL NAME** | *Aucuba japonica* |
| **FAMILY NAME** | *Cornaceae* |
| **COMMON NAME** | *Spotted laurel* |

**AVAILABILITY** ● Winter months.

**DESCRIPTION** ● Medium sized green oblong leaves with distinctive variegation born on branched stem.

**USES** ● Single leaves or stem as a whole, arrangements, baskets, pedestals.

**CARE POINTS** ● Re-cut stems & put into clean water, no additives.

| | |
|---|---|
| BOTANICAL NAME | *Azalea branches* |
| FAMILY NAME | *Rhododendron* |
| COMMON NAME | *Azalea branches* |

AVAILABILITY ● Winter months

DESCRIPTION ● Bare azalea branches
with natural lichen growing on it.

USES ● Line & texture emphasis, designer work only.

CARE POINTS ● Keep well misted until used.  Dries well.

# Bamboo

| | |
|---|---|
| **BOTANICAL NAME** | *Bamboo* |
| **FAMILY NAME** | *Bambuseae* |
| **COMMON NAME** | *Bamboo* |

**AVAILABILITY** ● All year

**DESCRIPTION** ● Long green tubular stems intersperced with circular nodes every 30cm or so.
Length & width variable.

**USES** ● Designer work, large displays, oriental & exotic scenes.

**CARE POINTS** ● Keep dry & covered. Will eventually change colour.

| BOTANICAL NAME | *Banana leaves* |
| FAMILY NAME | *Musaceae* |
| COMMON NAME | *Banana leaves* |

| AVAILABILITY | ● | All year |
| DESCRIPTION | ● | Large green oval shaped single leaves. 70-75cm long, 40-50cm wide |
| USES | ● | Large arrangements, pedestals, designer work, tropical scenes. |
| CARE POINTS | ● | Keep misted, wrapped loosely in plastic. Keep in a cool place (5°C). Use promptly. |

# Berzelia lanuginosa

| | |
|---|---|
| **BOTANICAL NAME** | *Berzelia lanuginosa* |
| **FAMILY NAME** | *Cape Greens* |
| **COMMON NAME** | *Lanuginosa* |

**AVAILABILITY** ● All year except March

**DESCRIPTION** ● Lime green leather-like foliage with tiny bobbles on top of stem.

**USES** ● Arrangements, baskets, handtieds, wedding work, colour & texture emphasis.

**CARE POINTS** ● Re-cut & put into clean water.

| | |
|---|---|
| **BOTANICAL NAME** | *Berzelia squarrosa* |
| **FAMILY NAME** | *Cape Greens* |
| **COMMON NAME** | *Palacea* |

| | | |
|---|---|---|
| **AVAILABILITY** | ● | October - January |
| **DESCRIPTION** | ● | Heather-like foliage with a crown of medium sized bobbles, cream/grey in colour. |
| **USES** | ● | Colour & texture emphasis. |
| **CARE POINTS** | ● | Re-cut stems & put into clean water. |

| BOTANICAL NAME | *Brunia laevis* |
| --- | --- |
| FAMILY NAME | *Cape Greens* |
| COMMON NAME | *Silver brunei* |

| AVAILABILITY | ● | August - December |
| --- | --- | --- |
| DESCRIPTION | ● | Silver bobbles on scaly stem. |
| USES | ● | Texture & colour emphasis. |
| CARE POINTS | ● | Re-cut & put into clean water. |

| BOTANICAL NAME | *Bupleurum griffithii* |
|---|---|
| FAMILY NAME | *Umbelliferae* |
| COMMON NAME | *Bupleurum* |

| | |
|---|---|
| AVAILABILITY | ● All year except January |
| DESCRIPTION | ● Lime green flowerheads & leaves on multiple soft stems on the main stem. |
| USES | ● All floristry work. Spring arrangements. Colour emphasis. |
| CARE POINTS | ● Re-cut stems & put into clean water with flower food. Put in a cool ventilated but not drafty place. |

| | |
|---|---|
| **BOTANICAL NAME** | *Buxus sempervirens* |
| **FAMILY NAME** | *Buxaceae* |
| **COMMON NAME** | *Boxtree* |

| | | |
|---|---|---|
| **AVAILABILITY** | ● | July - May |
| **DESCRIPTION** | ● | Green, red, variegated.  Small evergreen leaves on woody stem.  Variegated box more compact.  'Red box' autumn colour yellow/orange. |
| **USES** | ● | All floristry work, good filler. |
| **CARE POINTS** | ● | Hardy - re-cut stems & put into clean water. |

| | |
|---|---|
| **BOTANICAL NAME** | *Calathea insignis* |
| **FAMILY NAME** | *Marantaceae* |
| **COMMON NAME** | *Rattlesnake plant* |

**AVAILABILITY** • All year

**DESCRIPTION** • Long oval shaped leaves, green with dark red-brown distinct markings along veins. Purple underside. 15-30cm long, 7cm wide.

**USES** • Work requiring line & colour emphasis, arrangements, baskets, wedding work.

**CARE POINTS** • Keep misted, loosely wrapped in plastic & in a cool place (5°C). Store upside down to avoid curling. Use promptly.

## Calathea ornata

| BOTANICAL NAME | *Calathea ornata* |
| FAMILY NAME | *Marnataceae* |
| COMMON NAME | *Calathea ornata* |

| AVAILABILITY | ● | All year |
| DESCRIPTION | ● | Green oval leaves with white & pink stripes along veins. Purple underside. 15-30 cm long. |
| USES | ● | Arrangements, baskets, wedding work, line & colour emphasis. |
| CARE POINTS | ● | Keep misted, loosely wrapped in plastic, in a cool place (5°C). Store upside down to avoid curling. Use promptly. |

| | |
|---|---|
| **BOTANICAL NAME** | *Camellia* |
| **FAMILY NAME** | *Theaceae* |
| **COMMON NAME** | *Common camellia* |

**AVAILABILITY** ● Winter months

**DESCRIPTION** ● Strong & glossy leaves on hardy woody stem.

**USES** ● All floristry work. Single leaves used for wedding work.

**CARE POINTS** ● Re-cut stems & put into clean water, no addtives.

## Cane palm

| | |
|---|---|
| **BOTANICAL NAME** | *Cane palm* |
| **FAMILY NAME** | *Palmae* |
| **COMMON NAME** | *Cane palm* |

| | | |
|---|---|---|
| **AVAILABILITY** | ● | All year |
| **DESCRIPTION** | ● | 1m long fronds, leaflets open spaced. |
| **USES** | ● | Bold & large arrangements, designer decoration. |
| **CARE POINTS** | ● | Keep misted, wrapped loosely in plastic. Put in a cool place (5°C). |

**Cannomois virgata**

| | |
|---|---|
| BOTANICAL NAME | *Cannomois virgata* |
| FAMILY NAME | *Gramineae* |
| COMMON NAME | *Bell reed* |

| | | |
|---|---|---|
| AVAILABILITY | ● | All year |
| DESCRIPTION | ● | Long strong grasses with seed pods on hulm |
| USES | ● | Handtieds, waterfalls & design, work. |
| CARE POINTS | ● | Dries well. Use promptly, seed pods will open. |

# *Caustis blakei*

| | |
|---|---|
| **BOTANICAL NAME** | *Caustis blakei* (Australia)<br>*Rhodocoma gigantea* (S Africa) |
| **COMMON NAME** | *Koala fern* |

| | | |
|---|---|---|
| **AVAILABILITY** | ● | All year |
| **DESCRIPTION** | ● | Soft long fir on wiry stems. |
| **USES** | ● | Designer work & fillers. |
| **CARE POINTS** | ● | Keep misted, wrapped loosely in plastic.<br>Keep in a cool place (5°C).<br>Use promptly. |

| | |
|---|---|
| BOTANICAL NAME | *Cladonia rangifera* |
| COMMON NAME | *Deer foot moss* |

| | | |
|---|---|---|
| AVAILABILITY | ● | All year |
| DESCRIPTION | ● | Grey-whitish fluffy looking moss. |
| USES | ● | Focal point, filler, for wet and dry work. |
| CARE POINTS | ● | Keep dry. |

# Cocculus laurifolius

| | |
|---|---|
| **BOTANICAL NAME** | *Cocculus laurifolius* |
| **FAMILY NAME** | *Menispermaceae* |
| **COMMON NAME** | *Cocculus* |

**AVAILABILITY** ● All year

**DESCRIPTION** ● Glossy oval shaped leaves on soft to medium woody branch, 50 - 100cm in length.

**USES** ● Overarm bouquets, pedestals, waterfalls & all flowing-type floristry.

**CARE POINTS** ● Re-cut stems & put into clean water, no additives. Put in cool ventilated but not drafty place.

| | |
|---|---|
| BOTANICAL NAME | *Coco flex* |
| FAMILY NAME | *Cocos nucifera* |
| COMMON NAME | *Coconut palm* |

AVAILABILITY ● All year

DESCRIPTION ● Young leaves of coconut palm; large ovate green leaves 'pleated' veins, sail-like in appearance. 80cm long.

USES ● Modern arrangements, any work requiring large & distinctive leaves, designer work.

CARE POINTS ● Keep misted, wrapped loosely in plastic. Put in a cool place (5°C).

## Coco strips

| | |
|---|---|
| **BOTANICAL NAME** | *Coco strips* |
| **FAMILY NAME** | *Cocos nucifera* |
| **COMMON NAME** | *Coco strips* |

**AVAILABILITY** ● All year

**DESCRIPTION** ● Stripped palm buds with yellow centre & green outer edge. Very pliable. 1m length, 2.5cm wide.

**USES** ● Designer work, arrangements, decorative work.

**CARE POINTS** ● Keep misted, wrapped loosely in plastic.
Keep in a cool place (5°C).
Use promptly.

| BOTANICAL NAME | *Codiaeum* |
|---|---|
| FAMILY NAME | *Euphorbiacea* |
| COMMON NAME | *Croton* |

| | | |
|---|---|---|
| AVAILABILITY | ● | All year |
| DESCRIPTION | ● | Hardy, oval shaped colourful leaves, red, yellow & green, short stems. |
| USES | ● | Arrangements, baskets, wedding work. |
| CARE POINTS | ● | Keep misted, wrap loosely in plastic. Keep in a cool place (5°C). Use promptly. |

# Cordyline

| | |
|---|---|
| **BOTANICAL NAME** | *Cordyline* |
| **FAMILY NAME** | *Liliaceae* |
| **COMMON NAME** | *Ti plant* |

**AVAILABILITY** ● All year

**DESCRIPTION** ● Narrow long green leaves with stripes of cream, yellow, pink or red/maroon.

**USES** ● Line emphasis.

**CARE POINTS** ● Keep  misted, wrapped loosely in plastic.
Keep in a cool place (5°C).
Use promptly.

| BOTANICAL NAME | *Cornus* |
|---|---|
| FAMILY NAME | *Cornaceae* |
| COMMON NAME | *Dogwood, red & yellow* |

| AVAILABILITY | ● | Winter only |
|---|---|---|
| DESCRIPTION | ● | Bare woody stems, 1 m - 1.5 m in length, used for its colour in winter |
| USES | ● | Linear work. |
| CARE POINTS | ● | Re-cut stems & put into clean water, no additives. |

## Corylus avellana

| | |
|---|---|
| **BOTANICAL NAME** | *Corylus avellana* |
| **FAMILY NAME** | *Betulaceae* |
| **COMMON NAME** | *Hazel catkins* |

| | | |
|---|---|---|
| **AVAILABILITY** | ● | Early spring |
| **DESCRIPTION** | ● | Long catkins on bare stems. |
| **USES** | ● | Spring arrangements, handtieds. |
| **CARE POINTS** | ● | Re-cut stems & put into clean water, no additives.  Put in a cool ventilated but not drafty place.  Use promptly. Pollen can develop. |

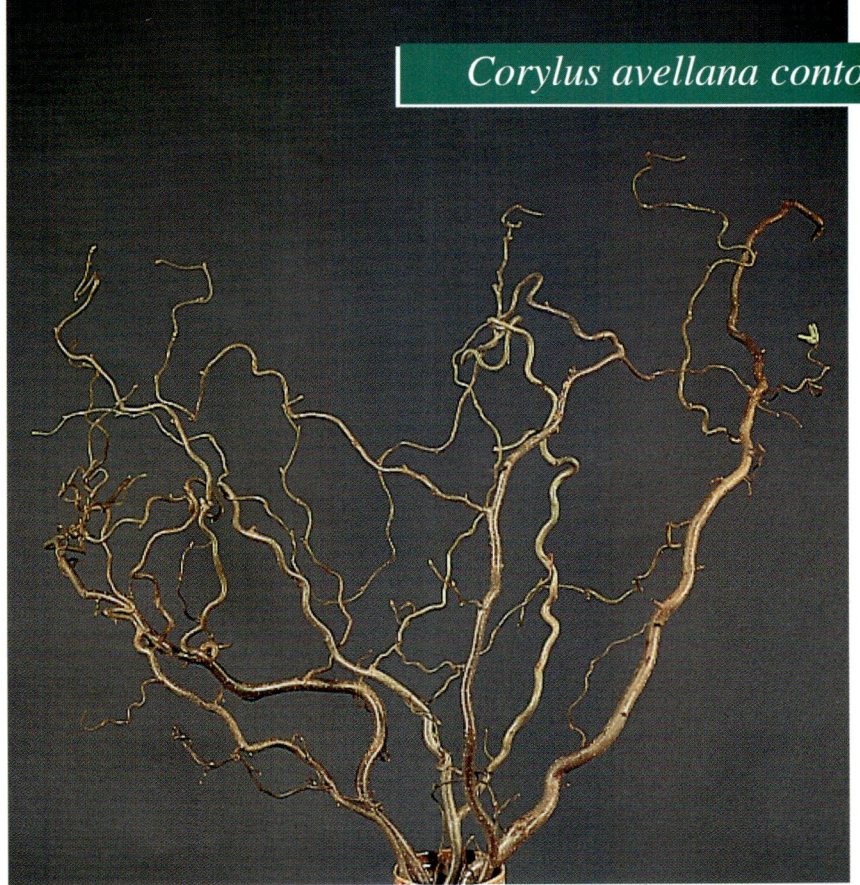

| BOTANICAL NAME | *Corylus avellana contorta* |
| FAMILY NAME | *Betulaceae* |
| COMMON NAME | *Contorted hazel, Corkscrew hazel* |

| AVAILABILITY | ● | Winter months |
| DESCRIPTION | ● | 30cm - 200cm in length. |
| USES | ● | Designer work, handtieds, pedestals & modern arrangements. |
| CARE POINTS | ● | Keep from drying out. |

**Cotinus**

| | |
|---|---|
| BOTANICAL NAME | *Cotinus* |
| FAMILY NAME | *Anacardiaceae* |
| COMMON NAME | *Smoke tree* |

AVAILABILITY ● Summer months.

DESCRIPTION ● Dark-brown/red round leaves on woody stem.

USES ● For its colour, pedestals, arrangements, handties.

CARE POINTS ● Re-cut stems & put into clean water, no additives. Put in a cool ventilated but not drafty place. Use promptly.

| | |
|---|---|
| **BOTANICAL NAME** | *Cotoneaster 'Cornubia'* |
| **FAMILY NAME** | *Rosaceae* |
| **COMMON NAME** | *Cotoneaster* |

| | | |
|---|---|---|
| **AVAILABILITY** | ● | September - April |
| **DESCRIPTION** | ● | Autumn foliage. |
| **USES** | ● | Pedestals, arrangments. |
| **CARE POINTS** | ● | Re-cut & put into clean water. |

| BOTANICAL NAME | *Cupressus* |
|---|---|
| FAMILY NAME | *Cupressaceae* |
| COMMON NAME | *Green & golden cupressus* |

| AVAILABILITY | ● | All year |
|---|---|---|
| DESCRIPTION | ● | Green cupressus & cupressus with yellow tips. |
| USES | ● | All floristry work, mainly funeral work. |
| CARE POINTS | ● | Re-cut stems & put into clean water, no additives. |

| | |
|---|---|
| **BOTANICAL NAME** | *Cycas revoluta* |
| **FAMILY NAME** | *Palmae* |
| **COMMON NAME** | *Cycas palm* |

| | | |
|---|---|---|
| **AVAILABILITY** | ● | All year |
| **DESCRIPTION** | ● | Small oblong palm leaves, rather stiff in appearance.  50cm long. |
| **USES** | ● | Arrangements, baskets. |
| **CARE POINTS** | ● | Keep cool and dry. |

# Cyperus papyrus

| | |
|---|---|
| **BOTANICAL NAME** | *Cyperus papyrus* |
| **FAMILY NAME** | *Cyperaceae* |
| **COMMON NAME** | *Papyrus* |

| | | |
|---|---|---|
| **AVAILABILITY** | ● | All year |
| **DESCRIPTION** | ● | Grassy tufts on strong stem. |
| **USES** | ● | Design work. |
| **CARE POINTS** | ● | Re-cut stems & put into clean water, no additives. Put in a cool ventilated but not drafty place. |

| BOTANICAL NAME | *Cyrtomium falcatum* |
| FAMILY NAME | *Polypodiaceae* |
| COMMON NAME | *Holly fern* |

| AVAILABILITY | ● | All year |
| DESCRIPTION | ● | Holly shaped leaflets on flowing stem. |
| USES | ● | Arrangements, baskets & funeral work. |
| CARE POINTS | ● | Keep misted, wrap loosely in plastic. Put in a cool place (5°C) |

## Cytisus / Genista

| | |
|---|---|
| **BOTANICAL NAME** | *Cytisus / Genista* |
| **FAMILY NAME** | *Leguminosae* |
| **COMMON NAME** | *Broom* |

| | | |
|---|---|---|
| **AVAILABILITY** | ● | Winter months |
| **DESCRIPTION** | ● | Long & thin, bare & green pliable branches up to 1m in length. |
| **USES** | ● | Arrangements, handtieds, pedestals, wedding & designer work. |
| **CARE POINTS** | ● | Re-cut stems & put into clean water, no additives. |

| | |
|---|---|
| **BOTANICAL NAME** | *Danae racemosa (Ruscus racemosa)* |
| **FAMILY NAME** | *Liliaceae* |
| **COMMON NAME** | *Soft Ruscus* |

| | | |
|---|---|---|
| **AVAILABILITY** | ● | All year. |
| **DESCRIPTION** | ● | Small slightly weavy green leaves on green stem. |
| **USES** | ● | All floristry work & garlands. |
| **CARE POINTS** | ● | Keep misted, wrap loosely in plastic. Keep in a cool place (5˚C). |

## Diosma subulata

| | |
|---|---|
| **BOTANICAL NAME** | *Diosma subulata* |
| **FAMILY NAME** | *Cape Greens* |
| **COMMON NAME** | *Diosma* |

| | |
|---|---|
| **AVAILABILITY** | ● October - April |
| **DESCRIPTION** | ● Green heather-like foliage. |
| **USES** | ● Arrangements, baskets, weddings, texture emphasis. |
| **CARE POINTS** | ● Re-cut & put into clean water. |

*Dodonea viscosa*

| | |
|---|---|
| **BOTANICAL NAME** | *Dodonea viscosa* |
| **FAMILY NAME** | *Sapindaceae* |
| **COMMON NAME** | *Dodonea* |

**AVAILABILITY** ● All year

**DESCRIPTION** ● Small leaves on woody stem, purple/copper coloured leaves in autumn & winter, getting lighter & greener in summer.

**USES** ● Arrangements, handtieds, pedestals, good filler.

**CARE POINTS** ● Re-cut stems & put into clean water, no additives. Put in a cool ventilated but not drafty place. Dries well.

# Dracaena masangeana

BOTANICAL NAME — *Dracaena masangeana*

FAMILY NAME — *Liliaceae*

COMMON NAME — *Dracaena masangeana*

AVAILABILITY ● All year

DESCRIPTION ● Long broad blade-like leaves with creamy stripe in the middle.

USES ● Line emphasis, weddings, handtieds, arrangements & baskets.

CARE POINTS ● Keep misted, wrapped loosely in plastic.
Keep in a cool place (5°C).
Use promptly.

| | |
|---|---|
| BOTANICAL NAME | *Dracaena sanderiana* |
| FAMILY NAME | *Liliaceae* |
| COMMON NAME | *Dracaena sanderiana* |

| | | |
|---|---|---|
| AVAILABILITY | ● | All year |
| DESCRIPTION | ● | Long green leaves with cream edge. |
| USES | ● | Line emphasis, arrangements, baskets, wedding work. |
| CARE POINTS | ● | Keep misted, wrapped loosely in plastic. Keep in a cool place (5°C). Use promptly. |

# Eleagnus

| | |
|---|---|
| **BOTANICAL NAME** | *Eleagnus* |
| **FAMILY NAME** | *Elaeagnaceae* |
| **COMMON NAME** | *Eleagnus* |

**AVAILABILITY** ● September - March

**DESCRIPTION** ● Green or green/yellow variegated oval shaped leaves on short stems - 30cm. Silver-grey underside.

**USES** ● All floristry work either as branch or single leaves.

**CARE POINTS** ● Re-cut stems & put into clean water, no additives. Put in a cool ventilated but not drafty place.

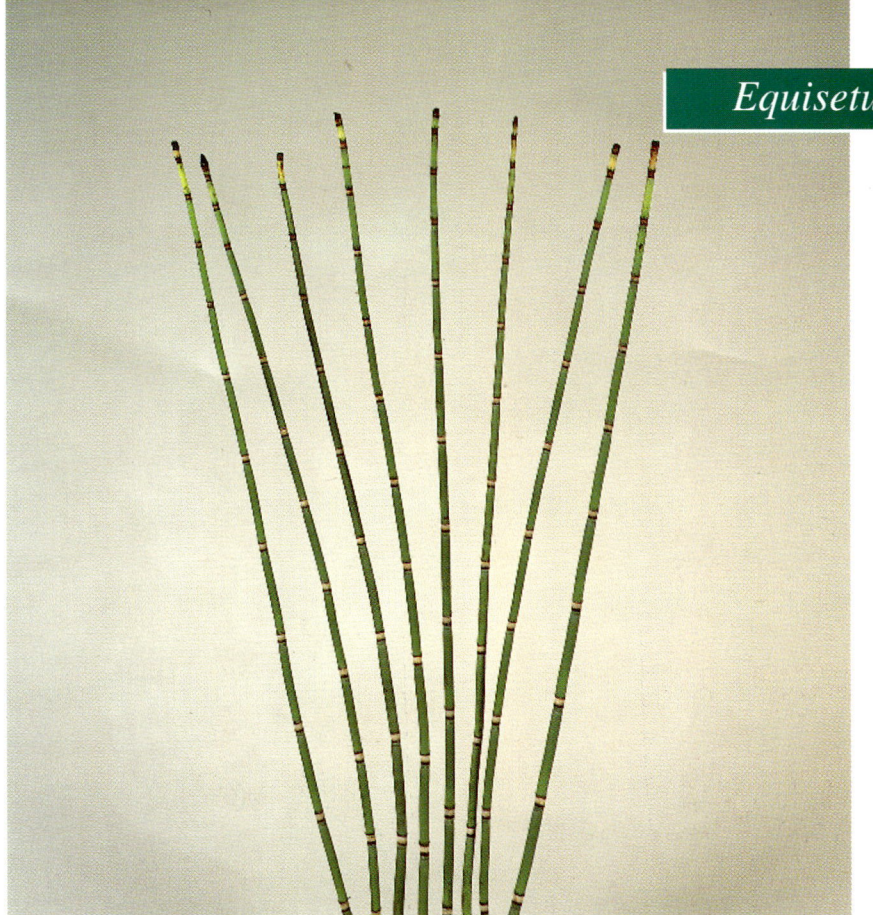

| | |
|---|---|
| **BOTANICAL NAME** | *Equisetum* |
| **FAMILY NAME** | *Equisetaceae* |
| **COMMON NAME** | *Snake grass* |

| | | |
|---|---|---|
| **AVAILABILITY** | ● | September - April |
| **DESCRIPTION** | ● | Long thin & hollow green stems with dark nodule markings. |
| **USES** | ● | Designer work. |
| **CARE POINTS** | ● | Keep misted, wrap loosely in plastic. Put in a cool place (5°C). |

# Erica plukenetti

| | |
|---|---|
| **BOTANICAL NAME** | *Erika plukenetti* |
| **FAMILY NAME** | *Ericaceae* |
| **COMMON NAME** | *Plukenetti* |

| | | |
|---|---|---|
| **AVAILABILITY** | ● | Jan - March |
| **DESCRIPTION** | ● | Green heather with lime green flowers. |
| **USES** | ● | Handtieds, arrangements, baskets, weddings, posies & texture use. |
| **CARE POINTS** | ● | Re-cut stems & put into clean water. |

| | |
|---|---|
| **BOTANICAL NAME** | *Escallonia* |
| **FAMILY NAME** | *Escalloniaceae* |
| **COMMON NAME** | *Escallonia* |

| | | |
|---|---|---|
| **AVAILABILITY** | ● | Winter months |
| **DESCRIPTION** | ● | Small glossy leaves on long woody stem. |
| **USES** | ● | Handtieds & pedestals.. |
| **CARE POINTS** | ● | Re-cut & put into clean water, no additives. |

# *Eucalyptus acaciaformis*

| | |
|---|---|
| BOTANICAL NAME | *Eucalyptus acaciaformis* |
| FAMILY NAME | *Myrtaceae* |
| COMMON NAME | *Acaciaformis* |

| | | |
|---|---|---|
| AVAILABILITY | ● | September - April |
| DESCRIPTION | ● | Long slender green leaves on slender red stem. |
| USES | ● | Flowing movement, waterfalls, arrangements, handtieds & designer work. |
| CARE POINTS | ● | Re-cut stems & put into clean water, no additives. Put in a cool ventilated but not drafty place. Use promptly. |

| | |
|---|---|
| **BOTANICAL NAME** | *Eucalyptus 'baby blue'* |
| **FAMILY NAME** | *Myrtaceae* |
| **COMMON NAME** | *Baby blue* |

| | | |
|---|---|---|
| **AVAILABILITY** | ● | October - March |
| **DESCRIPTION** | ● | Small blue-grey round leaves. Attached irregularly to grey stem. |
| **USES** | ● | Designer & wedding work, arrangements, baskets & posies. |
| **CARE POINTS** | ● | Re-cut stems & put into clean water, no additives. Put in a cool ventilated but not drafty place. |

# Eucalyptus camphora

| BOTANICAL NAME | *Eucalyptus camphora* |
| --- | --- |
| FAMILY NAME | *Myrtaceae* |
| COMMON NAME | *Camphora* |

| AVAILABILITY | ● | Winter months |
| --- | --- | --- |
| DESCRIPTION | ● | Heart shaped leaves. |
| USES | ● | Could be used for Valentine's Day arrangements. |
| CARE POINTS | ● | Re-cut stems & put into clean water, no additives.  Put in a cool ventilated but not drafty place. |

| | |
|---|---|
| **BOTANICAL NAME** | *Eucalyptus cinerea* |
| **FAMILY NAME** | *Myrtaceae* |
| **COMMON NAME** | *Cinerea* |

**AVAILABILITY** ● August - June

**DESCRIPTION** ● Round silver-grey leaves, 3cm - 4cm in length on woody stem.

**USES** ● All floristry work, good filler & good colour.

**CARE POINTS** ● Re-cut stems & put into clean water, no additives.  Put in a cool ventilated but not drafty place.

# *Eucalyptus coccifera*

| | |
|---|---|
| **BOTANICAL NAME** | *Eucalyptus coccifera* |
| **FAMILY NAME** | *Myrtaceae* |
| **COMMON NAME** | *Coccifera* |

| | | |
|---|---|---|
| **AVAILABILITY** | ● | Winter months |
| **DESCRIPTION** | ● | Long lancelot grey-green leaves on whitish stem, hence the name snow gum. Sometimes with flower buds. |
| **USES** | ● | Designer work, handtieds, arrangments & waterfalls. |
| **CARE POINTS** | ● | Re-cut stems & put into clean water, no additives. Put in a cool ventilated but not drafty place. |

| | |
|---|---|
| **BOTANICAL NAME** | *Eucalyptus dried bark* |
| **FAMILY NAME** | *Myrtaceae* |
| **COMMON NAME** | *Dried bark* |

| | | |
|---|---|---|
| **AVAILABILITY** | ● | Winter months |
| **DESCRIPTION** | ● | Wide strips of pliable brown bark. |
| **USES** | ● | Designer work. |
| **CARE POINTS** | ● | Prevent from drying out completly. Before use, spray to make more pliable. |

# Eucalyptus 'flower buds'

| | |
|---|---|
| **BOTANICAL NAME** | *Eucalyptus 'flower buds'* |
| **FAMILY NAME** | *Myrtaceae* |
| **COMMON NAME** | *Euco buds* |

| | | |
|---|---|---|
| **AVAILABILITY** | ● | October - January |
| **DESCRIPTION** | ● | Distinctive flowerbuds on bare stems, usually grey-green in colour. |
| **USES** | ● | Arrangements, baskets, handtieds, designer & wedding work, different texture. |
| **CARE POINTS** | ● | Prevent from drying out. |

| | |
|---|---|
| **BOTANICAL NAME** | *Eucalyptus glaucesens* |
| **FAMILY NAME** | *Myrtaceae* |
| **COMMON NAME** | *Glaucesens* |

**AVAILABILITY** ● September - April

**DESCRIPTION** ● Grey-blue round leaves with aromatic scent.

**USES** ● All floristry work.

**CARE POINTS** ● Re-cut stems & put into clean water, no additives. Put in a cool ventilated but not drafty place.

# Eucalyptus gunnii

| | |
|---|---|
| **BOTANICAL NAME** | *Eucalyptus gunnii* |
| **FAMILY NAME** | *Myrtaceae* |
| **COMMON NAME** | *Gunnii* |

**AVAILABILITY** ● August - May

**DESCRIPTION** ● Round silver-grey leaves, 1cm in length, on woody stem.

**USES** ● All floristry work, good filler & good for use of colour.

**CARE POINTS** ● Eucalyptus enjoys a growing period May to August. During that time the tips are soft and often 'burnt' by cold cold winds or late frost. It only hardens off in September and is hardy until next spring. Not recommended as a "standby" during May-August.

**Eucalyptus johnsonii**

| | |
|---|---|
| BOTANICAL NAME | *Eucalyptus johnsonii* |
| FAMILY NAME | *Myrtaceae* |
| COMMON NAME | *Johnsonii* |

| | | |
|---|---|---|
| AVAILABILITY | ● | September - May |
| DESCRIPTION | ● | Glossy oval green leaves on stem. Leaves 3cm - 5cm and hardy. |
| USES | ● | All floristry work, good filler. |
| CARE POINTS | ● | Re-cut & put into clean water (Hardy). |

| | |
|---|---|
| **BOTANICAL NAME** | *Eucalyptus nicoli* |
| **FAMILY NAME** | *Myrtaceae* |
| **COMMON NAME** | *Nicoli* |

| | | |
|---|---|---|
| **AVAILABILITY** | ● | August - May |
| **DESCRIPTION** | ● | Long thin leaves on slender stem. Soft in appearance. |
| **USES** | ● | Arrangements, handtieds, pedestals, flowing, trailing & wedding work. Waterfalls. |
| **CARE POINTS** | ● | Eucalyptus enjoys a growing period May to August. During that time the tips are soft and often 'burnt' by cold cold winds or late frost. It only hardens off in September and is hardy until next spring. Not recommended as a "standby" during May-August. |

*Eucalyptus parvifolia*

| | |
|---|---|
| **BOTANICAL NAME** | *Eucalyptus parvifolia* |
| **FAMILY NAME** | *Myrtaceae* |
| **COMMON NAME** | *Parvifolia* |

**AVAILABILITY** ● August - May

**DESCRIPTION** ● Small oval green leaves directly on stem.

**USES** ● All floristry work.

**CARE POINTS** ● Eucalyptus enjoys a growing period May to August. During that time the tips are soft and often 'burnt' by cold cold winds or late frost. It only hardens off in Aug/Sept and is hardy until next spring. Not recommended as a "standby" during May-August.

## Eucalyptus periniana

| | |
|---|---|
| **BOTANICAL NAME** | *Eucalyptus periniana* |
| **FAMILY NAME** | *Myrtaceae* |
| **COMMON NAME** | *Spinning Gum* |

| | | |
|---|---|---|
| **AVAILABILITY** | ● | Sept - Jan |
| **DESCRIPTION** | ● | Silver grey big round leaves attached to stem. |
| **USES** | ● | Designer work. |
| **CARE POINTS** | ● | Re-cut and put in clean water, out of draft, no flower food. |

| | |
|---|---|
| **BOTANICAL NAME** | *Eucalyptus populus* |
| **FAMILY NAME** | *Myrtaceae* |
| **COMMON NAME** | *Populus* |

**AVAILABILITY** ● August - April

**DESCRIPTION** ● Roundish grey-green leaves on its own stem coming from main stem.

**USES** ● Arrangements, handtieds, pedestals, designer work.

**CARE POINTS** ● Re-cut and put in clean water, out of draft, no flower food.

*Eucalyptus stuartiana*

| | |
|---|---|
| **BOTANICAL NAME** | *Eucalyptus stuartiana* |
| **FAMILY NAME** | *Myrtaceae* |
| **COMMON NAME** | *Stuartiana* |

**AVAILABILITY** ● July - May

**DESCRIPTION** ● Grey-green round leaves (3 - 4cm) with a point, attached on a stem.

**USES** ● All floristry work.

**CARE POINTS** ● Eucalyptus enjoys a growing period May to August. During that time the tips are soft and often 'burnt' by cold cold winds or late frost. It only hardens off in Aug/Sept and is hardy until next spring. Not recommended as a "standby" during May-August.

| | |
|---|---|
| BOTANICAL NAME | *Eucalyptus subcrenulata* |
| FAMILY NAME | *Myrtaceae* |
| COMMON NAME | *Subcrenulata* |

| | | |
|---|---|---|
| AVAILABILITY | ● | Winter months |
| DESCRIPTION | ● | A hardy glossy green leaved foliage. |
| USES | ● | Good filler, all floristry work. |
| CARE POINTS | ● | Re-cut stems & put into clean water, no additives. |

| | |
|---|---|
| **BOTANICAL NAME** | *Euonymus* |
| **FAMILY NAME** | *Celastraceae* |
| **COMMON NAME** | *Euonymus* |

**AVAILABILITY** ● All year

**DESCRIPTION** ● Green or variegated. Small green/or green-yellow variegated leaves on usually yellow stems. Lengths up to 75cm.

**USES** ● Handtieds, arrangements, pedestals & where variegated foliage is required.

**CARE POINTS** ● Re-cut stems & put into clean water, no additives. Put in a cool ventilated but not drafty place.

| | |
|---|---|
| **BOTANICAL NAME** | *Ficinea* |
| **FAMILY NAME** | *Gramineae* |
| **COMMON NAME** | *Braids* |

**AVAILABILITY** ● August - March

**DESCRIPTION** ● Platted reed grass approx. 2cm in width & 40cm in length.

**USES** ● Headdresses, baskets & wallhangings.

**CARE POINTS** ● Keep misted, wrapped loosely in plastic. Put in a cool place (5°C).

# *Galax viceolata*

| | |
|---|---|
| **BOTANICAL NAME** | *Galax viceolata* |
| **FAMILY NAME** | *Diapeusiaceae* |
| **COMMON NAME** | *Beetle weed* |

**AVAILABILITY** ● All year

**DESCRIPTION** ● Round shaped leaves, 3 - 9cm ,
green in spring & summer, and dark red to
mottled in autumn & winter.

**USES** ● Bridal and funeral work, modern
arrangements & underlining design.

**CARE POINTS** ● Keep misted, wrap loosley in plastic.
Put in a cool place (5°C).

| | |
|---|---|
| **BOTANICAL NAME** | *Gaultheria shallon* |
| **FAMILY NAME** | *Ericaceae* |
| **COMMON NAME** | *Salal, Salal tips* |

| | | |
|---|---|---|
| **AVAILABILITY** | ● | July  - June |
| **DESCRIPTION** | ● | Hardy medium sized leaves on woody stem, fan shaped branches.  Salal tips - smaller. |
| **USES** | ● | Arrangements, handtieds, pedestals, funeral work. |
| **CARE POINTS** | ● | Keep misted & wrapped in plastic (5°C). |

| | |
|---|---|
| **BOTANICAL NAME** | *Gleichenia polypodiodes* |
| **FAMILY NAME** | *Gleicheniaceae* |
| **COMMON NAME** | *Coral fern* |

| | | |
|---|---|---|
| **AVAILABILITY** | ● | March - December |
| **DESCRIPTION** | ● | Open-fan shaped fern. |
| **USES** | ● | Weddings, handtieds, posies, special emphasis. |
| **CARE POINTS** | ● | Keep misted, wrapped loosley in plastic. Keep in a cool place (5°C). Use promptly. Dries well. |

| | |
|---|---|
| **BOTANICAL NAME** | *Grevillea* |
| **FAMILY NAME** | *Proteaceae* |
| **COMMON NAME** | *Grevillea* |

**AVAILABILITY** ● September - May

**DESCRIPTION** ● Long serrated leaves on grey stem. Blue-grey underneath and green on top.

**USES** ● Most floristry work, handties, pedestals & flowing lines.

**CARE POINTS** ● Re-cut stems & put into clean water, no additives. Put in a cool ventilated but not drafty place.

# Grimmia pulvinata

| | |
|---|---|
| **BOTANICAL NAME** | *Grimmia pulvinata* |
| **FAMILY NAME** | *Cyrptogamia* |
| **COMMON NAME** | *Bun moss* |

**AVAILABILITY** ● All year

**DESCRIPTION** ● Round mounds of moss.

**USES** ● Basework.

**CARE POINTS** ● Keep moist.

| | |
|---|---|
| BOTANICAL NAME | *Hedera* |
| FAMILY NAME | *Araliaceae* |
| COMMON NAME | *Ivy, green & variegated* |

| | | |
|---|---|---|
| AVAILABILITY | ● | All year |
| DESCRIPTION | ● | Trailing strands of ivy leaves green or variegated. Strands up to 1m in length. |
| USES | ● | All flowing, trailing work, weddings, arrangements, waterfalls, pedestals & baskets. |
| CARE POINTS | ● | Keep misted, wrapped loosely in plastic. Keep in a cool place (5°C). Use promptly. |

## Hosta crispula

| | |
|---|---|
| **BOTANICAL NAME** | *Hosta crispula* |
| **FAMILY NAME** | *Liliaceae* |
| **COMMON NAME** | *Hosta leaves* |

| | |
|---|---|
| **AVAILABILITY** | ● June - July |
| **DESCRIPTION** | ● Medium sized single leaves, green, white, variegated edge. |
| **USES** | ● Summer arrangements, baskets, pedestals. |
| **CARE POINTS** | ● Re-cut stems & put into clean water with flower food. |

| | |
|---|---|
| **BOTANICAL NAME** | *Hypericum* |
| **FAMILY NAME** | *Hypericaceae* |
| **COMMON NAME** | *Hypericum* |

**AVAILABILITY** ● June - December

**DESCRIPTION** ● Branched brown-green multiple seedhead on stem with green leaves.

**USES** ● Filler & texture.

**CARE POINTS** ● Re-cut stems & put into clean water, no additives. Put in a cool ventilated but not drafty place. Use promptly.

| | |
|---|---|
| BOTANICAL NAME | *Ilex* |
| FAMILY NAME | *Ilicineae* |
| COMMON NAME | *Holly* |

AVAILABILITY ● December

DESCRIPTION ● Dark green or variegated glossy leaves. Some with prickles. Some with red or yellow berries.

USES ● Christmas work, holly wreaths.

CARE POINTS ● Keep cool & dry.

| | |
|---|---|
| **BOTANICAL NAME** | *Kochia* |
| **FAMILY NAME** | *Chenopodiaceae* |
| **COMMON NAME** | *Summer Cypress, Mock cypress* |

| | | |
|---|---|---|
| **AVAILABILITY** | ● | August - September |
| **DESCRIPTION** | ● | Long stems of bushy summer foliage. |
| **USES** | ● | All floristry work. |
| **CARE POINTS** | ● | Re-cut stems & put into clean water, no additives.  Put in a cool ventilated but not drafty place. |

# *Laurus nobilis*

| | |
|---|---|
| **BOTANICAL NAME** | *Laurus nobilis* |
| **FAMILY NAME** | *Lauraceae* |
| **COMMON NAME** | *Sweet bay, bay laurel* |

**AVAILABILITY** ● All year

**DESCRIPTION** ● Grey-green, hardy, aromatic leaves (herb used in cooking) on woody stem.

**USES** ● Filler. Arrangements, baskets, pedestals. Bushy foliage used for restaurant decoration. Can be used dried.

**CARE POINTS** ● Re-cut stems & place into clean water, no additives.

| | |
|---|---|
| BOTANICAL NAME | *Leptospermum* |
| FAMILY NAME | *Myrtaceae* |
| COMMON NAME | *Teetree* |

| | | |
|---|---|---|
| AVAILABILITY | ● | September - December |
| DESCRIPTION | ● | Tiny, delicate looking leaves on thin woody stems. |
| USES | ● | All floristry & designer work, line emphasis. |
| CARE POINTS | ● | Re-cut stems & put into clean water, no additives. Put in a cool ventilated but not drafty place. |

# Leucadendron argenteum

| | |
|---|---|
| BOTANICAL NAME | *Leucadendron argenteum* |
| FAMILY NAME | *Proteaceae* |
| COMMON NAME | *Silver tree* |

| | | |
|---|---|---|
| AVAILABILITY | ● | All year |
| DESCRIPTION | ● | Beautiful silver-grey foliage covering single stems - 40cm in length. |
| USES | ● | Designer work. |
| CARE POINTS | ● | Re-cut & put into clean water.  No additives |

| BOTANICAL NAME | *Leucadendron laureolum* |
| FAMILY NAME | *Proteaceae* |
| COMMON NAME | *Safari sunset* |

| AVAILABILITY | ● | January - July |
| DESCRIPTION | ● | Stem covered with lancelot leaves - green turning red further up the stem. |
| USES | ● | Colour & texture emphasis. |
| CARE POINTS | ● | Re-cut & put into clean water, no additives. |

# Leucadendron nervosum

| | |
|---|---|
| **BOTANICAL NAME** | *Leucadendron nervosum* |
| **FAMILY NAME** | *Proteaceae* |
| **COMMON NAME** | *Nervosum male* |

**AVAILABILITY** ● Autumn

**DESCRIPTION** ● Roundish green leaves covering single stem.

**USES** ● Arrangements, handties requiring different texture.

**CARE POINTS** ● Re-cut & put into clean water. No additives.

| | |
|---|---|
| **BOTANICAL NAME** | *Leucadendron platyspermum* |
| **FAMILY NAME** | *Proteaceae* |
| **COMMON NAME** | *Platyspermum* |

| | | |
|---|---|---|
| **AVAILABILITY** | ● | All year except Jan |
| **DESCRIPTION** | ● | Yellow bushy foliage. |
| **USES** | ● | Arrangements, handtieds, colour emphasis. |
| **CARE POINTS** | ● | Re-cut & put into clean water. No additives. |

# *Leucadendron rubrum*

| BOTANICAL NAME | *Leucadendron rubrum* |
|---|---|
| FAMILY NAME | *Proteaceae* |
| COMMON NAME | *Plumosum* |

| AVAILABILITY | ● | January - December |
|---|---|---|
| DESCRIPTION | ● | Small delicate leaves on straight woody stem topped with delicate flower buds. |
| USES | ● | All floristry use. |
| CARE POINTS | ● | Re-cut & put into clean water. No additives. |

## Leucadendron salicifolium strictum

| | |
|---|---|
| **BOTANICAL NAME** | *Leucadendron salicifolium strictum* |
| **FAMILY NAME** | *Proteaceae* |
| **COMMON NAME** | *Strictum* |

| | | |
|---|---|---|
| **AVAILABILITY** | ● | November - April |
| **DESCRIPTION** | ● | Distinctive brown/green coloured cones along stem with small leaves. |
| **USES** | ● | Texture & colour emphasis. |
| **CARE POINTS** | ● | Re-cut & put into clean water. No additives. |

# Leucadendron salignum

| | |
|---|---|
| **BOTANICAL NAME** | *Leucadendron salignum* |
| **FAMILY NAME** | *Proteaceae* |
| **COMMON NAME** | *Red adscendens* |

| | |
|---|---|
| **AVAILABILITY** | ● August - November |
| **DESCRIPTION** | ● Red foliage like a flowerhead on a woody stem. |
| **USES** | ● Colour & texture emphasis. |
| **CARE POINTS** | ● Re-cut & put into clean water. No additives. |

## *Leucospermum trucatulum*

| | |
|---|---|
| **BOTANICAL NAME** | *Leucospermum trucatulum buxifolia* |
| **FAMILY NAME** | *Proteaceae* |
| **COMMON NAME** | *Buxifolia* |

| | | |
|---|---|---|
| **AVAILABILITY** | ● | All year |
| **DESCRIPTION** | ● | Long stems with scale-like leaves & fluffy tops. |
| **USES** | ● | Handtieds, arrangements, weddings, design work & texture emphasis. |
| **CARE POINTS** | ● | Re-cut & put into clean water.  Spray. Not suitable for flower foam.  Dries well. |

# *Ligularia*

| | |
|---|---|
| **BOTANICAL NAME** | *Ligularia* |
| **FAMILY NAME** | *Compositae* |
| **COMMON NAME** | *Ligularia* |

| | | |
|---|---|---|
| **AVAILABILITY** | ● | All year |
| **DESCRIPTION** | ● | Large round leaves.  70cm long incl stem, 40 cm in diameter, |
| **USES** | ● | Designer work. |
| **CARE POINTS** | ● | Keep misted, wrapped loosely in plastic. Keep in a cool place (5°C).  Use promptly. |

| | |
|---|---|
| **BOTANICAL NAME** | *Ligustrum* |
| **FAMILY NAME** | *Oleaceae* |
| **COMMON NAME** | *Privet* |

**AVAILABILITY** ● All year

**DESCRIPTION** ● Green or yellow small leaves on woody stem.

**USES** ● Filler foliage.

**CARE POINTS** ● Re-cut stems & put into clean water, no additives. Put in a cool ventilated but not drafty place. Use promptly.

| BOTANICAL NAME | *Liriope muscari* |
| --- | --- |
| FAMILY NAME | *Liliaceae* |
| COMMON NAME | *Lily grass, green & variegated* |

| AVAILABILITY | ● | All year |
| --- | --- | --- |
| DESCRIPTION | ● | 1 - 2cm in width and up to 50cm in length. This foliage is wider than Beargrass. |
| USES | ● | Weddings, smaller arrangements & baskets. |
| CARE POINTS | ● | Keep misted, wrapped loosely in plastic. Put in a cool place (5°C). |

| | |
|---|---|
| **BOTANICAL NAME** | *Melaleuca* |
| **FAMILY NAME** | *Myrtaceae* |
| **COMMON NAME** | *Melaleuca* |

| | | |
|---|---|---|
| **AVAILABILITY** | ● | All year |
| **DESCRIPTION** | ● | Gracious well covered stems by little light-green leaflets. |
| **USES** | ● | All floristry work, flowing lines. |
| **CARE POINTS** | ● | Re-cut stems & put into clean water, no additives.  Put in a cool ventilated but not drafty place. |

| | |
|---|---|
| **BOTANICAL NAME** | *Mercinia* |
| **FAMILY NAME** | *Africanaceae* |
| **COMMON NAME** | *Mercinia* |

| | | |
|---|---|---|
| **AVAILABILITY** | ● | All year |
| **DESCRIPTION** | ● | Small & neat round leaves on reddish stem. |
| **USES** | ● | All floristry work. |
| **CARE POINTS** | ● | Re-cut & put into clean water |

| | |
|---|---|
| BOTANICAL NAME | *Miscanthus sinensis variegatus / green* |
| FAMILY NAME | *Gramineae* |
| COMMON NAME | *China grass, variegated & green* |

| | | |
|---|---|---|
| AVAILABILITY | ● | All year |
| DESCRIPTION | ● | Widths are approx 1cm, length approx 35cm. |
| USES | ● | Arrangements, baskets, wedding work, posies. |
| CARE POINTS | ● | Wrap loosely in plastic & put in a cool place (5°C). |

| BOTANICAL NAME | *Molulcella laevis* |
|---|---|
| FAMILY NAME | *Labiatae* |
| COMMON NAME | *Bells of Ireland* |

| | | |
|---|---|---|
| AVAILABILITY | ● | All year |
| DESCRIPTION | ● | Rings of lime green bells on a green stem. |
| USES | ● | Weddings, handtieds, arrangements & designer work. |
| CARE POINTS | ● | Re-cut stems & put into clean water, no additives. Put in a cool ventilated but not drafty place. Use promptly. |

| | |
|---|---|
| **BOTANICAL NAME** | *Monstera deliciosa* |
| **FAMILY NAME** | *Araceae* |
| **COMMON NAME** | *Swiss cheese plant* |

**AVAILABILITY** ● All year

**DESCRIPTION** ● Medium to large single philodendron leaves.

**USES** ● Arrangements, handtieds, pedestals.

**CARE POINTS** ● Keep misted, wrapped loosely in plastic. Keep in a cool place (5°C).

# Moss branches

| | |
|---|---|
| **BOTANICAL NAME** | *Moss branches* |
| **FAMILY NAME** | |
| **COMMON NAME** | *Moss branches* |

| | | |
|---|---|---|
| **AVAILABILITY** | ● | All year |
| **DESCRIPTION** | ● | Woodland branches with hanging moss. |
| **USES** | ● | Large design work & window displays. |
| **CARE POINTS** | ● | None |

| BOTANICAL NAME | *Musci* |
|---|---|
| FAMILY NAME | *Bryophyte* |
| COMMON NAME | *Flat moss* |

| | | |
|---|---|---|
| AVAILABILITY | ● | All year |
| DESCRIPTION | ● | Carpet-like continuous moss. |
| USES | ● | Basing, filler. |
| CARE POINTS | ● | Keep sprayed. |

# Myrica gale

| | |
|---|---|
| **BOTANICAL NAME** | *Myrica gale* |
| **FAMILY NAME** | *Myricaceae* |
| **COMMON NAME** | *Sweet gale* |

**AVAILABILITY** ● February - April.

**DESCRIPTION** ● Bare Brown branches with flower buds on upper half. Stems between 50 & 75 cm in length..

**USES** ● Handties, arrangements & designer work.

**CARE POINTS** ● Re-cut stems & put into clean water, no additives. Put in a cool ventilated but not drafty place.

| | |
|---|---|
| **BOTANICAL NAME** | *Myrtus communis* |
| **FAMILY NAME** | *Myrtaceae* |
| **COMMON NAME** | *Myrtle* |

**AVAILABILITY** ● July - May

**DESCRIPTION** ● Small lancelot aromatic leaves on woody stems.

**USES** ● Suitable for all floristry work, very versatile filler foliage.

**CARE POINTS** ● Re-cut stems & put into clean water, no additives. Put in a cool ventilated but not drafty place.

## Nephrolepis exaltata

| | |
|---|---|
| **BOTANICAL NAME** | *Nephrolepis exaltata* |
| **FAMILY NAME** | *Oleandraceae* |
| **COMMON NAME** | *Sword fern / Washington fern* |

| | | |
|---|---|---|
| **AVAILABILITY** | ● | All year |
| **DESCRIPTION** | ● | Delicate & erect fern with small leaves. |
| **USES** | ● | Wedding work, small arrangements, funeral sprays, posies & baskets. |
| **CARE POINTS** | ● | Keep misted, wrapped loosely in plastic. Keep in a cool place (5°C).  Use promptly. |

| BOTANICAL NAME | *Olearia* |
| --- | --- |
| FAMILY NAME | *Compositae* |
| COMMON NAME | *Tree aster, Daisy bush* |

| | | |
| --- | --- | --- |
| AVAILABILITY | ● | Autumn / Winter |
| DESCRIPTION | ● | Grey-green serrated leaves on woody stem. |
| USES | ● | Branches used as filler, single leaves for buttonhole corsages etc |
| CARE POINTS | ● | Re-cut stems & put into clean water, no additives.  Put in a cool ventilated but not drafty place. |

# Paranomus

| | |
|---|---|
| **BOTANICAL NAME** | *Paranomus* |
| **FAMILY NAME** | *Proteaceae* |
| **COMMON NAME** | *Paranomus* |

**AVAILABILITY** ● June - September

**DESCRIPTION** ● Hardy, scaly leaves covering stem with white/pinkish flower.

**USES** ● Texture use & designer work.

**CARE POINTS** ● Re-cut & put into clean water. Dries well.

*Phormium tenax*

| | |
|---|---|
| **BOTANICAL NAME** | *Phormium tenax* |
| **FAMILY NAME** | *Liliaceae* |
| **COMMON NAME** | *New Zealand flax* |

| | | |
|---|---|---|
| **AVAILABILITY** | ● | All year |
| **DESCRIPTION** | ● | Long hardy lancealate sword-like leaves in either green, cream, variegated, purple or brown. |
| **USES** | ● | Arrangements, pedestals, design work & line emphasis. |
| **CARE POINTS** | ● | Keep misted, wrapped loosely in plastic. Put in a cool place (5°C). |

# *Picea abies*

| | |
|---|---|
| BOTANICAL NAME | *Picea abies* |
| FAMILY NAME | *Pinaceae* |
| COMMON NAME | *Norway spruce* |

| | | |
|---|---|---|
| AVAILABILITY | ● | November - January |
| DESCRIPTION | ● | Original Christmas tree foliage. Small needles all around stem. |
| USES | ● | Christmas work. |
| CARE POINTS | ● | Re-cut & put into water. |

*Pinus contorta latifolia*

| | |
|---|---|
| **BOTANICAL NAME** | *Pinus contorta latifola* |
| **FAMILY NAME** | *Pinaceae* |
| **COMMON NAME** | *Lodgepole pine/Tufty pine* |

| | | |
|---|---|---|
| **AVAILABILITY** | ● | November - January |
| **DESCRIPTION** | ● | Long needles on stem - giving an erect tufty appearance. |
| **USES** | ● | Christmas and designer work. |
| **CARE POINTS** | ● | Re-cut & put into clean water. |

# *Pistacia lentiscus*

| | |
|---|---|
| **BOTANICAL NAME** | *Pistacia lentiscus* |
| **FAMILY NAME** | *Anacardiaceae* |
| **COMMON NAME** | *Lentiscum* |

**AVAILABILITY** ● July - May

**DESCRIPTION** ● Leaves consist of leaflets on small branches on woody stems.

**USES** ● Branchlets can be taken for arrangements, main stem can be used for handtieds. Also used for baskets & all other floristry work.

**CARE POINTS** ● Re-cut stems & put into clean water, no additives. Put in a cool ventilated but not drafty place.

| | |
|---|---|
| **BOTANICAL NAME** | *Pittosporum* |
| **FAMILY NAME** | *Pittosporaceae* |
| **COMMON NAME** | *Pitto* |

**AVAILABILITY** ● August - April

**DESCRIPTION** ● Green: small slightly curly leaf
variegated: Silver Queen small slightly curly leaf.
variegated:Tobira broad leaf, forming rosette.

**USES** ● Filler & all floristry work.

**CARE POINTS** ● Re-cut stems & put into clean water, no additives.
Put in a cool ventilated but not drafty place.

# Pleomele thalioide

| | |
|---|---|
| **BOTANICAL NAME** | *Pleomele thalioide* |
| **FAMILY NAME** | *Pleomele* |
| **COMMON NAME** | *Thalioide leaves* |

**AVAILABILITY** ● All year

**DESCRIPTION** ● Elongated ovate leaves on long sturdy stem. Leaves notably veined.

**USES** ● Arrangements, handtied, baskets.

**CARE POINTS** ● Wrap loosely in plastic & put in a cool place (5°C).

| | |
|---|---|
| **BOTANICAL NAME** | *Podocarpus* |
| **FAMILY NAME** | *Podocarpaceae* |
| **COMMON NAME** | *Emu grass* |

**AVAILABILITY** ● All year

**DESCRIPTION** ● Long needle-like but soft leaves on dark-green stem.

**USES** ● Arrangements, baskets, posies & funeral work.

**CARE POINTS** ● Re-cut stems & put into clean water, no additives. Put in a cool ventilated but not drafty place.

# *Podocarpus nagi*

| | |
|---|---|
| BOTANICAL NAME | *Podocarpus nagi* |
| FAMILY NAME | *Taxaceae* |
| COMMON NAME | *Nagi* |

| | | |
|---|---|---|
| AVAILABILITY | ● | All year - scarce in summer. |
| DESCRIPTION | ● | Solid leaflets on branched stems. Hardy foliage. |
| USES | ● | All floristry work. |
| CARE POINTS | ● | Re-cut stems & put into clean water, no additives. Put in a cool ventilated but not drafty place. |

| | |
|---|---|
| **BOTANICAL NAME** | *Pokers* |
| **FAMILY NAME** | *Gramineae* |
| **COMMON NAME** | *Pokers* |

| | | |
|---|---|---|
| **AVAILABILITY** | ● | All year |
| **DESCRIPTION** | ● | Erect brownish pointed stems, with lengths up to 60cm. |
| **USES** | ● | Designer work. |
| **CARE POINTS** | ● | Keep dry. |

| | |
|---|---|
| **BOTANICAL NAME** | *Polystichum munitum* |
| **FAMILY NAME** | *Polypodiaceae* |
| **COMMON NAME** | *Flat fern* |

| | | |
|---|---|---|
| **AVAILABILITY** | ● | All year |
| **DESCRIPTION** | ● | Larger sword fern. |
| **USES** | ● | Arrangements, baskets, funeral sprays. |
| **CARE POINTS** | ● | Keep misted, wrapped loosely in plastic. Keep in a cool place (5°C).  Use promptly. |

| | |
|---|---|
| **BOTANICAL NAME** | *Prunus avium* |
| **FAMILY NAME** | *Rosaceae* |
| **COMMON NAME** | *Cherry branches* |

| | | |
|---|---|---|
| **AVAILABILITY** | ● | Early spring |
| **DESCRIPTION** | ● | Bare dark-brown branches with blossom buds. |
| **USES** | ● | Spring arrangements, handtieds. |
| **CARE POINTS** | ● | Re-cut stems & put into clean water, no additives. |

## Prunus laurocerasus

| | |
|---|---|
| **BOTANICAL NAME** | *Prunus laurocerasus* |
| **FAMILY NAME** | *Rosaceae* |
| **COMMON NAME** | *Common laurel* |

**AVAILABILITY** ● Winter months

**DESCRIPTION** ● Hardy, large glossy green oval shaped leaves on woody stem.

**USES** ● Pedestals, displays & backing of funeral sprays.

**CARE POINTS** ● Re-cut stems & put into clean water, no additives. Put in a cool ventilated but not drafty place.

| | |
|---|---|
| **BOTANICAL NAME** | *Rhapis Excelsa* |
| **FAMILY NAME** | *Palmaceae* |
| **COMMON NAME** | *Rapish palm* |

**AVAILABILITY** ● All year

**DESCRIPTION** ● Hand-sized & larger fan shaped palm. Wider leaves coming from middle attached to stem.

**USES** ● Arrangements, handtieds, wedding work.

**CARE POINTS** ● Keep misted, wrapped loosely in plastic. Put in a cool place (5°C).

# *Rosmarinus officinalis*

| | |
|---|---|
| **BOTANICAL NAME** | *Rosmarinus officinalis* |
| **FAMILY NAME** | *Labiatae* |
| **COMMON NAME** | *Rosemary* |

**AVAILABILITY** ● August - April

**DESCRIPTION** ● Grey-green stems covered with soft needles. Aromatic herb used in cooking.

**USES** ● Arrangements, baskets, posies, wedding work.

**CARE POINTS** ● Re-cut stems & put into clean water, no additives. Put in a cool ventilated but not drafty place.

| | |
|---|---|
| **BOTANICAL NAME** | *Rubus* |
| **FAMILY NAME** | *Rosaceae* |
| **COMMON NAME** | *Rubus* |

**AVAILABILITY** ● Summer-Autumn

**DESCRIPTION** ● Trailing furry stemmed foliage with glossy leaves.

**USES** ● As trailing foliage or single leaves for bridal work.

**CARE POINTS** ● Re-cut & put into clean water, keep wrapped and put in a cool place - tends to dry out if in a draft.

# *Ruscus hypoglossum*

| | |
|---|---|
| **BOTANICAL NAME** | *Ruscus hypoglossum* |
| **FAMILY NAME** | *Liliaceae* |
| **COMMON NAME** | *Hard Ruscus* |

---

**AVAILABILITY** ● All year

**DESCRIPTION** ● Strong green leaves attached to hard green stem.

**USES** ● All floristry work.

**CARE POINTS** ● Re-cut stems & put into clean water, no additives. Put in a cool ventilated but not drafty place.

| BOTANICAL NAME | *Sabal palmetto* |
| --- | --- |
| FAMILY NAME | *Palmaceae* |
| COMMON NAME | *Palm Buds* |

| AVAILABILITY | ● | All year |
| --- | --- | --- |
| DESCRIPTION | ● | Unopened palm that can be stripped to individual leaflets. 1.5m long. |
| USES | ● | Designer work. |
| CARE POINTS | ● | Keep dry |

*Salix fragilis*

| | |
|---|---|
| **BOTANICAL NAME** | *Salix fragilis* |
| **FAMILY NAME** | *Salicaceae* |
| **COMMON NAME** | *Pussy willow* |

| | | |
|---|---|---|
| **AVAILABILITY** | ● | February - March |
| **DESCRIPTION** | ● | White/grey catkins directly on bare, brown stem. |
| **USES** | ● | Arrangements, handtieds, baskets. |
| **CARE POINTS** | ● | Keep dry.  (In water, the 'pussies' will open & the stems start developing leaves)  Use promplty. |

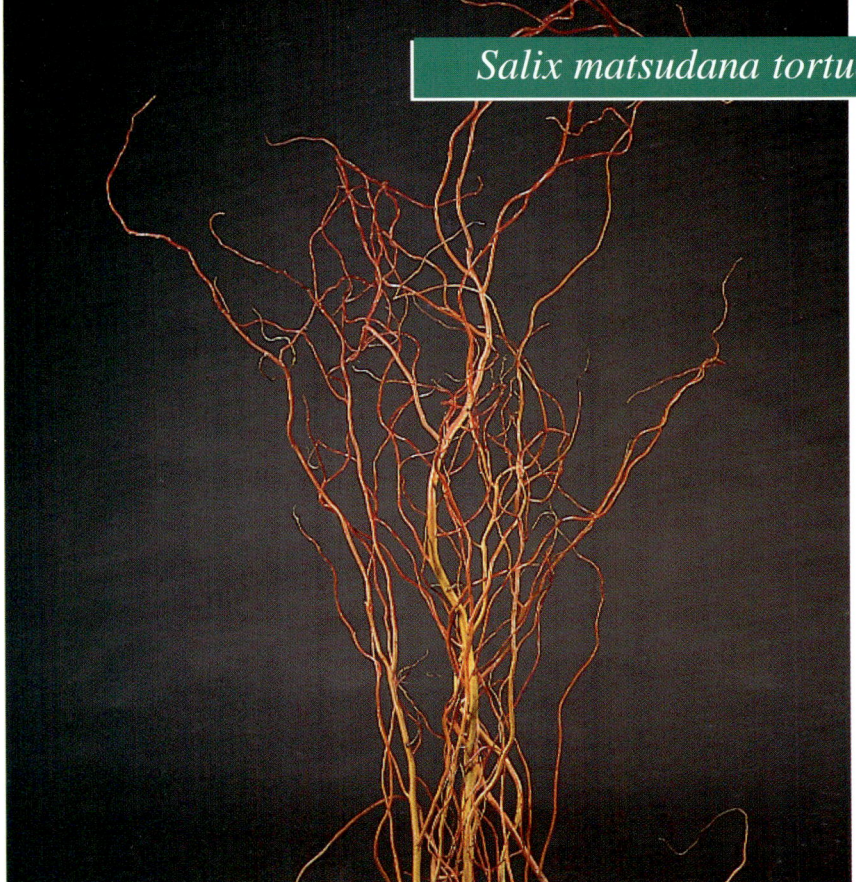

| BOTANICAL NAME | *Salix matsudana tortuosa* |
|---|---|
| FAMILY NAME | *Salicaceae* |
| COMMON NAME | *Contorted willow* |

| AVAILABILITY | ● | Autum to Spring |
|---|---|---|
| DESCRIPTION | ● | Twisted willow with lengths up to 2m. |
| USES | ● | Arrangements, handtieds, pedestals, designer work. |
| CARE POINTS | ● | To keep its suppleness, do not let it dry out. Keep it wrapped in plastic. |

# *Salix viminalis*

| | |
|---|---|
| **BOTANICAL NAME** | *Salix viminalis* |
| **FAMILY NAME** | *Salicaceae* |
| **COMMON NAME** | *Weaving willow* |

**AVAILABILITY** ● December - March

**DESCRIPTION** ● Slender, brown or yellow, sometimes with a tinge of red, pliable stems.

**USES** ● Designer work, weaving, bending, bundling.

**CARE POINTS** ● To keep its suppleness, do not let it dry out. Keep it wrapped in plastic.

## Scindapsus aureus

| | |
|---|---|
| **BOTANICAL NAME** | *Scindapsus aureus* |
| **FAMILY NAME** | *Araliaceae* |
| **COMMON NAME** | *Devils ivy* |

| | | |
|---|---|---|
| **AVAILABILITY** | ● | All year |
| **DESCRIPTION** | ● | Single medium sized green & cream variegated leaves. |
| **USES** | ● | Arrangements, basket, posies. |
| **CARE POINTS** | ● | Wrap in plastic & put in a cool ventilated but not drafty place. |

| | |
|---|---|
| **BOTANICAL NAME** | *Selaginella martensii* |
| **FAMILY NAME** | *Selaginellacea* |
| **COMMON NAME** | *Lycopodium/Club moss* |

| | | |
|---|---|---|
| **AVAILABILITY** | ● | All year |
| **DESCRIPTION** | ● | Delicate stems covered with scale - like small leaves. |
| **USES** | ● | Posies, Wedding work, small arrangements, different texture. |
| **CARE POINTS** | ● | Long lasting, keep moist. |

| | |
|---|---|
| **BOTANICAL NAME** | *Serenoa repens* |
| **FAMILY NAME** | *Palmaceae* |
| **COMMON NAME** | *Palm Fan* |

| | | |
|---|---|---|
| **AVAILABILITY** | ● | All year |
| **DESCRIPTION** | ● | Circular hard palm.  Leaves evenly bisected to form a full fan shape around 90cm. |
| **USES** | ● | Large arrangements, display & designer work. |
| **CARE POINTS** | ● | Keep misted, wrapped loosely in plastic. Put in a cool place (5°C). |

| | |
|---|---|
| **BOTANICAL NAME** | *Spagnaceae* |
| **FAMILY NAME** | *Bryophyte* |
| **COMMON NAME** | *Sphagnum Moss* |

| | | |
|---|---|---|
| **AVAILABILITY** | ● | All year |
| **DESCRIPTION** | ● | Strands of green-whitish moss. |
| **USES** | ● | Good for holding moisture in pots or baskets. |
| **CARE POINTS** | ● | Keep moist. |

| BOTANICAL NAME | *Spartium* |
| FAMILY NAME | *Leguminosae* |
| COMMON NAME | *Spanish Broom* |

| AVAILABILITY | ● | All year |
| DESCRIPTION | ● | Yellow bushy stems with sparse leaf growth. |
| USES | ● | Arrangements, handtieds, baskets, colour & line emphasis. |
| CARE POINTS | ● | Re-cut & put into clean water. |

# *Stephanandra tanake*

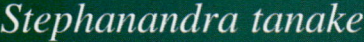

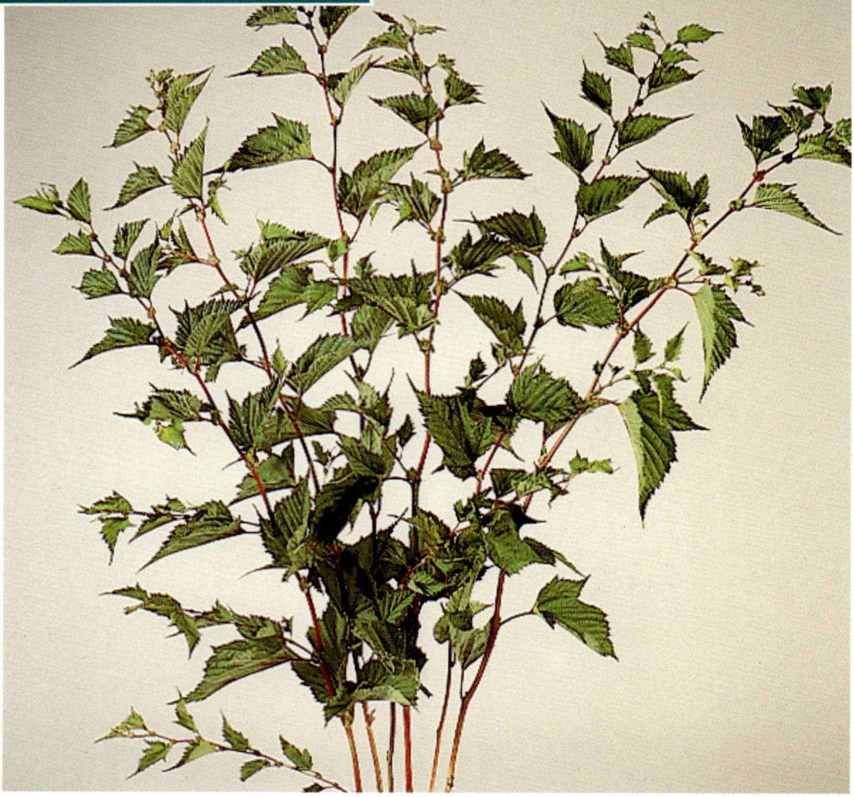

| | |
|---|---|
| BOTANICAL NAME | *Stephanandra tanake* |
| FAMILY NAME | *Rosaceae* |
| COMMON NAME | *Stephanandra* |

| | |
|---|---|
| AVAILABILITY | September - October |
| DESCRIPTION | Arching branches of autumn-shade foliage, usually 1m & longer in length. |
| USES | Large & small arrangements, design work, colour emphasis. |
| CARE POINTS | Re-cut stems & put into clean water, no additives. Put in a cool ventilated but not drafty place. Good laster if correctly treated. |

| | |
|---|---|
| **BOTANICAL NAME** | *Strelizia leaves* |
| **FAMILY NAME** | *Musaceae* |
| **COMMON NAME** | *Birds of Paradise leaves* |

| | | |
|---|---|---|
| **AVAILABILITY** | ● | All year |
| **DESCRIPTION** | ● | Hardy & strong elongated ovate erect green leaves on strong red veined stem. |
| **USES** | ● | Large arrangements & designer work. |
| **CARE POINTS** | ● | Keep in water & cool (5°C). |

# *Syngonium*

| BOTANICAL NAME | *Syngonium* |
| --- | --- |
| | *Araceae* |
| FAMILY NAME | *Goosefoot plant* |
| COMMON NAME | |

| | | |
| --- | --- | --- |
| AVAILABILITY | ● | All year |
| DESCRIPTION | ● | Small to medium sized leaves available. Oblong pointed at the front & back. Usually white veins in the middle of green leaves. |
| USES | ● | Colour texture & underlining work. |
| CARE POINTS | ● | Keep misted, wrapped loosely in plastic. Put in a cool place (5°C) |

| BOTANICAL NAME | *Thamnochortus insignis* |
|---|---|
| FAMILY NAME | *Gramineae* |
| COMMON NAME | *Shell reed* |

AVAILABILITY ● March - July

DESCRIPTION ● Long reed which rattles with its shell-like browny ends.

USES ● Designer work.

CARE POINTS ● Keep cool.

| | |
|---|---|
| **BOTANICAL NAME** | *Thuja* |
| **FAMILY NAME** | *Cupressaceae* |
| **COMMON NAME** | *Green cupressus* |

| | | |
|---|---|---|
| **AVAILABILITY** | ● | All year |
| **DESCRIPTION** | ● | Handy foliage. |
| **USES** | ● | Mainly funeral work. |
| **CARE POINTS** | ● | Re-cut & put into clean water |

| | |
|---|---|
| **BOTANICAL NAME** | *Tillandsia usenoides* |
| **FAMILY NAME** | *Bromeliadceae* |
| **COMMON NAME** | *Spanish Moss* |

**AVAILABILITY** ● All year

**DESCRIPTION** ● Long grey curly strands of narrow moss.

**USES** ● Waterfalls, trailing, wedding & design work.

**CARE POINTS** ● Keep wrapped loosely in plastic.
Keep in a cool place.

## Tsuga

| | |
|---|---|
| **BOTANICAL NAME** | *Tsuga* |
| **FAMILY NAME** | *Pinaceae* |
| **COMMON NAME** | *Hemlock* |

| | | |
|---|---|---|
| **AVAILABILITY** | ● | All year |
| **DESCRIPTION** | ● | Pine branches with flatish needles sometimes with small cones on ends. |
| **USES** | ● | Arrangements, baskets, funeral work, Christmas decorations. |
| **CARE POINTS** | ● | Re-cut stems & put into clean water, no additives. |

| | |
|---|---|
| **BOTANICAL NAME** | *Virburnum tinus* |
| **FAMILY NAME** | *Virburnum caprifoliceae* |
| **COMMON NAME** | *Virburnum* |

**AVAILABILITY** ● Summer - Autumn

**DESCRIPTION** ● Flower clusters in Spring, blue berries in Autumn, oblong veined green leaves.

**USES** ● Colour & texture requirements.

**CARE POINTS** ● Re-cut stems & put into clean water

# Virburnum grandiflorum

| | |
|---|---|
| **BOTANICAL NAME** | *Virburnum grandiflorum* |
| **FAMILY NAME** | *Caprifoliaceae* |

| | | |
|---|---|---|
| **AVAILABILITY** | ● | December - April |
| **DESCRIPTION** | ● | Flower clusters flushed with pink, dark green leaves. |
| **USES** | ● | All floristry work. |
| **CARE POINTS** | ● | Re-cut stems & put into clean water |

| | |
|---|---|
| **BOTANICAL NAME** | *Vaccinium ovatum* |
| **FAMILY NAME** | *Ericaceae* |
| **COMMON NAME** | *Huckleberry, green or red* |

| | | |
|---|---|---|
| **AVAILABILITY** | ● | August - April |
| **DESCRIPTION** | ● | Small green leaves on stem, strong branches. Red - tinged leaves on red barked stem. |
| **USES** | ● | All floristry work. |
| **CARE POINTS** | ● | Re-cut stems & put into clean water, no additives. Put in a cool ventilated but not drafty place. |

# Xanthorrhoea australis

| | |
|---|---|
| **BOTANICAL NAME** | *Xanthorrhoea australis* |
| **FAMILY NAME** | *Liliaceae* |
| **COMMON NAME** | *Steel Grass* |

| | | |
|---|:---:|---|
| **AVAILABILITY** | ● | All year |
| **DESCRIPTION** | ● | Up to 2 m long strong grass |
| **USES** | ● | Pedestals, large displays & designer work. |
| **CARE POINTS** | ● | Keep cool & prevent from drying out. |

| | |
|---|---|
| **BOTANICAL NAME** | *Xerophyllum tenax* |
| **FAMILY NAME** | *Liliaceae* |
| **COMMON NAME** | *Beargrass* |

**AVAILABILITY** ● All year

**DESCRIPTION** ● Long grassy leaves ranging between 30 & 90 cm. in length. Also available dried & coloured.

**USES** ● All floristry work, line emphasis.

**CARE POINTS** ● Keep misted, wrapped loosely in plastic, put in a cool place (5°C).

*...ia floridana*

**BOTANICAL NAME**    *Zamia floridana*

**FAMILY NAME**    *Cycadaceae*

**COMMON NAME**    *Coontie fern*

---

**AVAILABILITY** ●   All year

**DESCRIPTION** ●   Strong fern.

**USES** ●   Arrangements, baskets, handtieds, pedestals, funeral sprays.

**CARE POINTS** ●   Re-cut stems & put into clean water, no additives. Put in a cool well ventilated but not drafty place.

---